First published in the United Kingdom in 2020 by Pavilion
43 Great Ormond Street
London
WC1N 3HZ

ISBN 9781911641100

A CIP catalogue record for this book is available
from the British Library.

10 9 8 7 6 5 4 3 2 1

Reproduction by Rival Colour Ltd, UK
Printed and bound by 1010 Printing International Limited

www.pavilionbooks.com

CATH KIDSTON

A PLACE CALLED HOME

Photography by
Christopher Simon Sykes

PAVILION

Welcome

Introduction

'When we walked in I had that heart-stopping moment when I felt I could have been at home, and the feeling completely overtook me.'

For fifteen years my husband, Hugh, and I lived in a beautiful old 17th-century farmhouse in a magical spot up a valley in Gloucestershire. It faced south, had a pretty terraced garden, and a glorious view across rolling countryside that was a patchwork of woods and meadows. But I had had a feeling for quite a few years that it was not the house that I wanted to grow old in. It had steep winding stairs, and rather small windows which all looked one way, there being none at the back of the house, and our sitting room only had windows down one side. It just wasn't quite right, and though we had looked at ways of improving it and had drawn up plans to make some changes, it was going to be a lot of work. I had been brought up in a house that was light and airy – a bright, sunny, and cheerful home, where all the inspiration for my work stemmed from. I secretly longed to be back in a house that had that feeling of airiness, which might be somewhere that I would want to stay forever.

I am the sort of person who finds it very hard to walk past an estate agent's window without stopping to have a look, and I would get magazines every week to see what was for sale. I also made poor Hugh drive miles and miles around the countryside looking at houses. Though I loved the area, I didn't think we'd find the kind of house I was looking for – Cotswolds homes tend to be small and pretty. One day, however, a copy of *Country Life* landed on our doorstep. Browsing through it, I came across some stunning photographs of a house sitting on the edge of a valley, which turned out to be just below where we had walked our dogs for years. Not one of our walks had ever taken us past this house; it's tucked away and almost invisible, so we had never known it existed.

Standing in a valley, the Cotswolds house was called Paradise, as romantic a name as one could wish for. It had probably been a modest farmhouse – one of many in the area, which had been at the centre of sheep farming in the 17th century. Then a wealthy merchant bought and enlarged it, and over the years other owners had added on to it, turning it into the rambling manor house it is today. We went to look at it, and when we arrived it was pouring with rain and was a really miserable day, but when we walked in I had that heart-stopping moment when I felt I could have been at home, and the feeling completely overtook me. The people who were living there had been there since

the 1970s and hadn't modernised it in the way that makes houses lose their character – it had all the old floors, fireplaces, sinks and cupboards, and was totally unspoilt. Being quite impatient people we both just thought: 'Let's move.'

When we first moved in, of course I was thinking about decoration and how everything would work, and my main thought was that I wanted to settle in a house that would stay the way it was for our lifetime. I didn't want it to be marked by what was fashionable that year. For practical and financial reasons, I wanted to accommodate as many of the belongings that we had brought with us as possible. But I also knew that we would have to buy some new things and get rid of some other things. That is how I started to think about it, as if I were putting together a giant jigsaw puzzle.

For a year, while the builders were working on the structure, we lived in the cottage at the back. The house did need modernising in the sense that it had to be rewired and replumbed. It also needed a new roof, but apart from that there was very little structural work. We did open it up a bit, because the previous owners had used the top floor as a flat, which they had let to tenants, while the extension at the back was let separately as the cottage. Basically, we put it back to how it would have been as a merchant's house. Where there were more bedrooms than we needed, we turned some of them into bathrooms. Then, when the builders finally left, we moved in pretty quickly and began to put the jigsaw together.

We had a lot of furniture and stuff in storage. Some of it was from Hugh's London house, which I had decorated – a job that had led to us getting together. Some of it came from my parents' house in Wales. After my mother died, I had a lot of furniture left to me, such as a little four-poster bed that I had slept in as a child, and which is now in a room at the top of the house. Then there were dozens of paintings, many of them left to me by my great-aunt, Corise, a wonderful artist whom I adored. She left my sister and I the entire collection of her paintings, which was really important to us.

We were lucky to have inherited so much stuff from various members of the family. When Aunt Serena died, for example, she left her nieces and nephews all of her treasures. She had the most

incredible home, an old Rectory in Wiltshire, a beautiful house the decoration of which she had made her life's work. She had very traditional English country-house things. She died just before we moved into this house, and it was most peculiar because the huge club fender that she left us perfectly fitted the fireplace here – it was like it had been made for it. Things just seemed to land in place when they arrived.

I also inherited a lot from my beloved younger brother, Geordy. I had once helped him to decorate his London flat and his cottage in the country. Geordy was something of a magpie, and when he very sadly died three years ago, he left me some of his amazing collection of pictures, as well as more furniture inherited from our parents. So with all these rather old-fashioned things that I had inherited, I tried to layer on things that would make them feel a bit more up-to-date.

Then there was the garden to consider. The house we had come from had a complicated garden with lots of terraces, and it had been very high maintenance. When we arrived here, and I realised that we were probably going to grow old

in this house, I knew we had to keep the garden very simple. There is nothing worse when you are old than fighting a complicated garden. The previous owners had had no interest whatsoever in gardening, and only really had a bit of lawn, so it was a blank canvas.

One of the reasons I fell in love with the house was the incredible view down the valley, and I felt we didn't need much more. The garden already had an orchard, so we added wildflowers and planted lots more trees. I love having flowers in the house, so we also made a cutting garden and put in a greenhouse so I could grow geraniums. Scented geraniums are something of an obsession of mine – I'm not a very good gardener but I can grow geraniums. So there are geraniums almost all the year round to put in the house.

I do very much remember as a child there always being flowers in the house, and being encouraged by my mother to go and pick them, and to take an interest in them. I remember, too, that my nightdress had rosebuds on it. My mother gave us all our own patch of garden in which to grow whatever we wanted, and I grew flowers in mine. To this day, the first thing I do when I arrive home from a trip away is go and pick flowers to put in the house.

I cannot resist floral things. Before I became a decorator, I worked with an antique textile dealer. They used to sell old coats from the Middle East and on the back, or in the lining, there were often amazing chintzes. This gave me a love of floral fabrics, and of pattern and print (plus a sense of what worked well together), and this interest lead to me having the idea for what would become my signature style.

When I was in my 30s, I had a lot of friends who were getting married, moving house, and having children. They didn't necessarily have much money and they probably had their grandmother's chest of drawers and a few other bits and pieces to muddle together. As they couldn't afford to have a modern, slick house, I had the notion of opening a glorified junk shop that would be filled with household goods bought from car boot sales. And that's what I did. I also sold plastic tablecloths, so if you had a smart table you could put one over the top and the children could make as much mess as they liked. Then I made an ironing board cover with flowers

on it and people went crazy for it – those things just didn't exist at the time. This was the start of Cath Kidston.

We were careful when we restored the building that we didn't change the character too much, as I loved the way it was so unspoilt. We were very fortunate to have some wonderful builders who specialised in restoring historic houses. Dave Savage, the foreman who is now a great friend, had an amazing eye for detail. We didn't need an architect with him in charge. I could sketch something on the back of an envelope and he could translate it into a working drawing. He and his team ensured that all the restoration was pretty much invisible.

When we bought the house called Paradise, it was in the period not long after I had left the company. For the first time in all of my adult life I was not working, and I was free to think about the house and focus on it. It was an amazing time because it was a great distraction and I was able to think about what I wanted next. I knew I wanted new things, but I also wanted some of my Cath Kidston memories. These were the hopes that shaped what we have done.

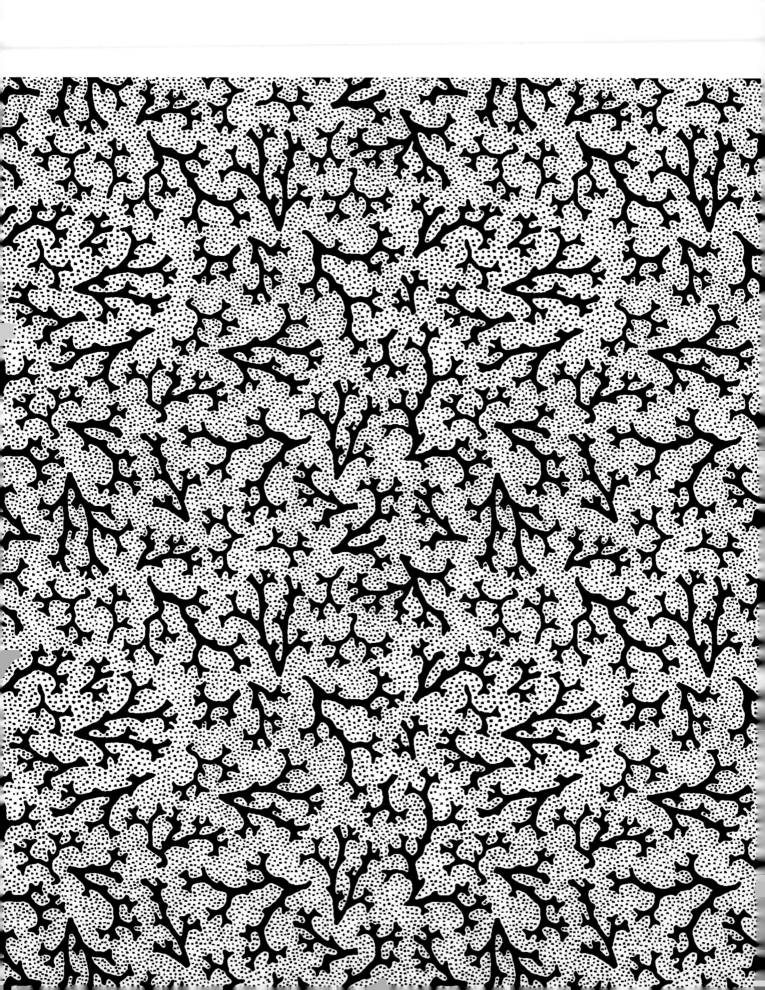

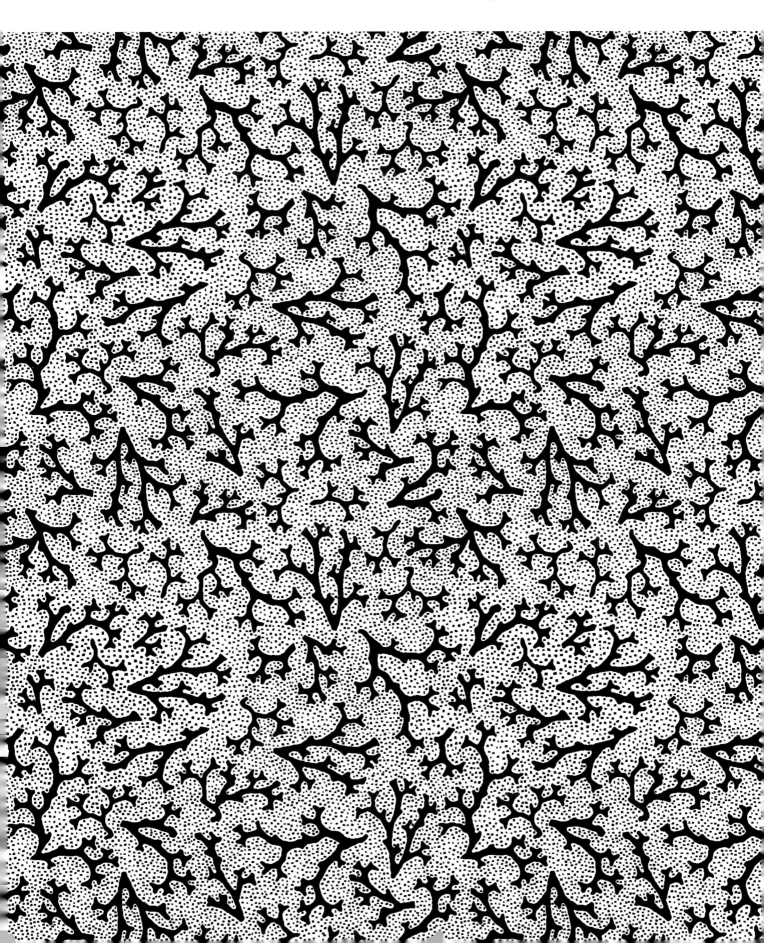

DELIVERIES &
COTTAGE WING →

'Our approach to the ground floor was all about bringing light in. We didn't have to change much of its structure, so it felt quite easy.'

When we first arrived, the ground floor was quite dark and serious, and we immediately decided that we must try and get a feeling of light flowing through it. So we added a glass door at the far end that opened out onto the terrace, creating a view right through from the front door to the garden. This meant that in the summer, guests could come in the entrance hall, walk right through the inner hall and go straight out into the garden. In fact, one of the first things I always do when I arrive home from London is to open all the doors up and let in as much light as possible.

From the beginning I knew that I wanted the ground floor to be calmer and less crowded than the rest of the house. I had decided that most of the very colourful things that I owned would be put upstairs, keeping the ground floor not too fussy and not too feminine. Here I could put a lot of the black and white things, and some old brown furniture that I wanted to use. I wanted to make the bones of the rooms feel quite plain with light colours and lots of white. This would suit the high ceilings in the house, which we love having, and which is something you don't get in many houses around here. We also improved the skylight above the staircase.

For new visitors, the layout of the ground floor can seem complicated because you can wander round and round and think you're completely lost until you find yourself back where you started. Around the part of the hall where the staircase is, I thought the pillars might make it feel a little bit old-fashioned and pompous, so rather than just having one big picture on the wall, I hung my collection of colourful prints up the stairs to make it feel less serious.

I think the overall feeling of the ground floor is simplicity. I also wanted it to be friendly when you walked in, so in the winter we have a lovely big fire in the entrance hall, which is very inviting when people arrive. Then there is the drinks table beside the staircase, so you go from the fire, to the drinks tray, to the cosiness in the telly room. It is a very welcoming entrance, which is just what I felt when I first walked through the front door.

Entrance Hall

'The front door opens in two, so my favourite thing in the summer is to fling both doors open, which makes the house much more welcoming.'

The entrance hall has remained exactly as it was. It is somewhere for people to dump their coats, and also acts as a draft-stopper for the rest of the house in that it is a sort of lobby before you come through the door into the inner hall. Otherwise it is just passed through when people come in and out or use the downstairs loo that sits off it. Therefore I have kept it very simple, with whitewashed walls, a plain tin overhead lantern, and a plain black bench. The only colour is a splash of red in the small Moroccan rug on the old flagstone floor. I was recently given a lovely small antique marble-topped table that fits perfectly in the corner, which I throw my keys on when I come in. There is, of course, a giant dog bowl to let people know that this is a dog-friendly home.

Though I tried to resist hanging too many pictures here, I quite like seeing some things I love when I walk through the front door, such as one of my favourite dog pictures and a few black-and-white prints. There are also a couple of barometers that I have inherited along the way. My late brother left me a beautiful Ravilious engraving of a farmyard, which hangs in the corner. It is a lovely reminder of him when I arrive home.

OPPOSITE A cracker hat hides the bald patch on this old portrait. It was put there one Christmas but never taken down as he looks so much happier with it on.

Sitting Room

'I remember looking around the house for the first time and being entranced walking into this room, with its three lovely long windows that flooded it with light.'

The sitting room is off the entrance hall and faces down the valley. The rooms are very different on this side of the house as a new front was added on the south side in the 18th century. The owner at that time had travelled to America and returned with the notion of making the house grander, so he elongated the sash windows and added in the Gothic panes. I remember looking around the house for the first time and being entranced by this room, with its three lovely long windows that flooded it with light.

The striking feature of the room is the beautiful fireplace, the design of which was made to mirror the ornate, carved stone arch that sits above the French windows on the outside of the building. When open, the windows lead out into the garden on the south side of the house. On either side of the chimneypiece hang two Dutch panels that originally belonged to my parents, and which I bought from my brother. They now fit there perfectly, but for ages I had nothing over the fireplace itself because its shape made it hard to know what to put there. Then I came across this really beautiful bronze branch by Dan Chadwick. It was made at the Pangolin foundry, who have a gallery near here, and it turned out to be just right for the space.

OPPOSITE I love collecting white china. This elephant lamp is Italian and one of a precious pair.

This room has three south-facing windows and a fantastic view of the valley. I procrastinated for ages over the colour I should paint it, trying endless samples on the walls, until one day, when I had a deadline for a photoshoot, I opted for my default pale blue from the local shop. I kept meaning to change it as I had chosen it on impulse, but so many people say how much they like it, it will probably stay this way. I wanted this room to be calmer than the telly room, so I found a very faded old rug in the local auction house that you don't really notice and built the colours around that – like the Howard material in pale green and white on the sofas, and the plain linen curtains. I then added a few splashes of yellow and extra colours in the cushions and the pictures.

We come in here when we have friends over or a houseful of guests. The room is a good shape for plenty of seating, which was important when I planned the layout. As people naturally gravitate towards the fireplace, the main group of sofas and chairs are at that end of the room, along with a huge stool for people to perch on or put down their drinks. There's also a sofa and a couple of chairs at the far end.

The furniture in the room is quite traditional, mainly pieces I already had, but we also added a pair of modern floating bookshelves and some contemporary pictures into the mix. I like the different styles together and will keep looking for some more modern pieces.

OPPOSITE The needlework cushion is made by prisoners for the charity Fine Cell Work, and was designed by Ben Pentreath. The red embroidered cushion is an old favourite from William Yeoward.

'The striking feature of the room is the beautiful fireplace, the design of which was made to mirror the ornate, carved stone arch that sits above the French windows on the outside of the building.'

Inner Hall

'It's amazing how these old pieces
of furniture are so adaptable, and
luckily back in fashion.'

'The large mirror helps to exaggerate the space and brings more light into the room. I usually have pots of geraniums scattered about to add a bit of green.'

The inner hall is the centre of the house, with a wide, open staircase lit by a large skylight on the first-floor landing. It's a lovely double-height space, and looked quite grand when we arrived, with big dark oil paintings and a pair of stone pillars at the base of the stairs. Double doors lead in to it from the entrance hall, and it has a good feeling of space that is rather a surprise as you enter. It was painted orange when we arrived and I wanted to lighten it up, so decided to paint it all white.

Realising we had no single picture with enough presence to hang in the stairway, I decided instead to place my favourite colourful prints all the way up the main wall. I included everything from a Damien Hirst to a £20 poster I bought online. They are such an eclectic mix, with lots of reds and yellows, and they were quite difficult to arrange. There is still one gap I am waiting to fill, but the colourful gallery wall has definitely brought the hall into the 21st century. The rest of the walls in the inner hall are hung with mainly black-and-white pictures. There is a large mirror over a bookcase, which helps exaggerate the space and brings some more light into the room, and I usually have large pots of geraniums scattered about to add a bit of green.

OPPOSITE The walls in the hall are painted our own house white. It is pure white with a small tint of black to take the brightness out. We have used this mix throughout the house.

We inherited a parquet floor that I restored and have laid with red Moroccan rugs, while the stairway itself now has a beautiful Swedish, yellow-and-white carpet, making it all feel much lighter. I used a large mahogany table inherited from my parents to make a drinks table under the stairs. I laid a piece of petrol-blue glass on top of it, which lightens it up, but is also practical and fun. It's amazing how these old pieces of furniture are so adaptable, and luckily back in fashion.

The stairs open up onto the first-floor landing. I built a large bookcase across the back wall, because I can never have too many bookshelves, and for a bit of contrast I put a modern tomato-red table in front of it. On the floor I was able to use my favourite Moroccan rug, which is pink and green and embroidered with teapots. It somehow links the two floors together.

It was difficult to find a large enough lantern to hang over the stairwell. Though I searched endlessly, I couldn't find one with the right character. In the end, I used three large classic paper lanterns, grouped like a bunch of balloons. They hang on red cord and, I think, make the hall.

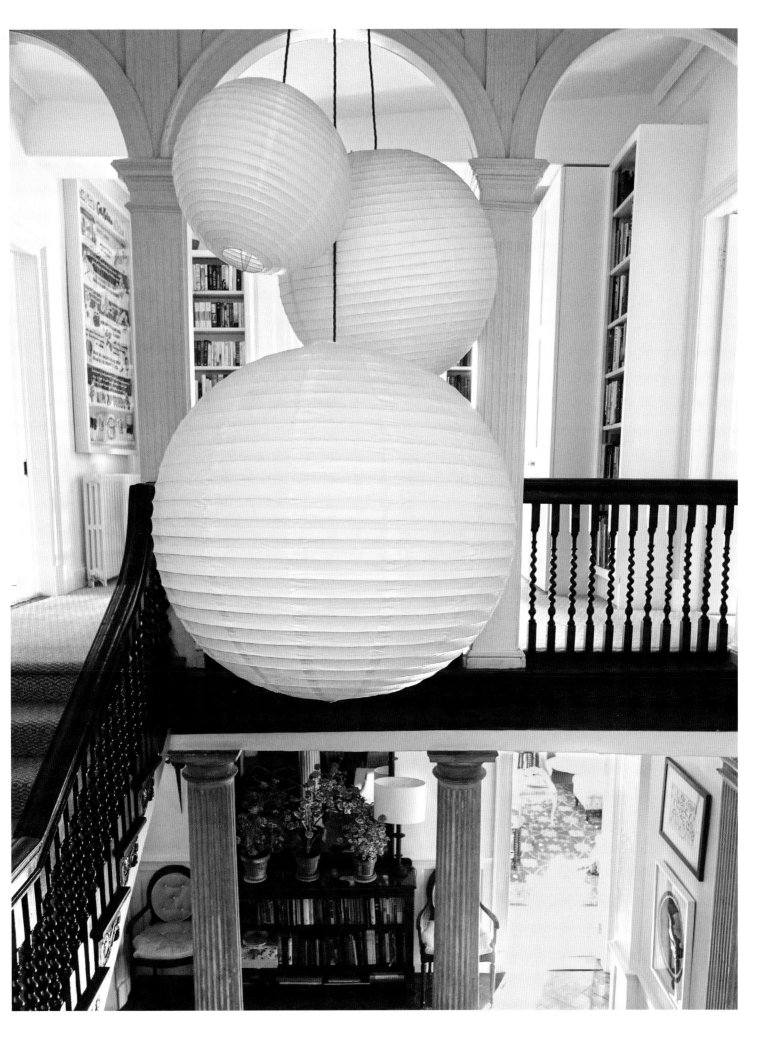

Telly Room

This is the room in which we spend as much time as we do in the kitchen. It's the telly room, the reading room, and the lounging-around room for both people and dogs. It's really comfortable and relaxed, a very cosy space that we use every day when it's just us, or if we have a couple of friends staying. It basically contains the contents of our old house. I found the rug, for example, for Hugh when I was working as his decorator. It is Persian and we bought it in a shop in London on the Wandsworth Bridge Road. I had to work hard to persuade him to buy it, which he did very grudgingly...

The contents of the room are a real junk shop mix. A lot of the furniture came from car boot sales because when we were at our old farmhouse I used to go every Sunday to the car boot in Gloucester to buy stock for my shop. Then there are the pictures inherited from my great-aunt, Corise, the artist. She was a great character, and a lot of her paintings are hanging in this room, pictures that I have known all my life. I loved her house and her use of reds, yellows, and blues (quite childish colours in a way), which are reflected in the decoration here. They are a combination I come back to again and again.

It is a very pretty room with a lovely fireplace. It has Gothic windows and lights on both sides, and being a corner room it gets the sun all day. In the summer, with its white walls, it is light and fresh. While in the winter, with the shutters closed and a fire in the grate, it is snug and inviting. It is a room that is very much about comfort and mood. It is very friendly. People come in and immediately feel at home. You can put your feet up. The dogs are usually asleep on the sofa, or more often than not, sitting with us watching telly. It is a relaxed living room, very much based around the unifying palette of the soft reds, yellows and blues of the rug, which makes it feel calm. Though there is quite a lot in it, it is still quite simple. The rug is the anchor for the room and everything fits together around it.

The room did present one challenge, and that was where to put the telly. Hugh and I can never agree about this, and in our last house we ended up with an enormous screen on one side of the fireplace, which I hated. Luckily, here there was a perfect blank wall behind the door and that is where we put it, making it in effect hidden. I was able to put a pair of large, very comfy armchairs opposite, each with stools, so for once we were both happy.

'I have enjoyed the puzzle of making use of the things I had, and the chance to move them on a bit and make them look different.'

One of the challenges of moving house when you are a bit older is the amount of stuff you have already accumulated – furniture and pictures and this and that. Though I got rid of some pieces that didn't feel as if they fitted in or suited the house, I have also enjoyed the puzzle of making use of the things I had, and the chance to move them on a bit and make them look different. So this room has come together with a mix of what I already had, plus a few new paintings, and white walls to keep it plain. Though there is a sentimental side to things, I am also trying to make the house chic, pretty, and cheerful as well. It's about trying to strike the right balance – giving the room a sense of fun, energy, and modernity, while using all these treasured old things.

OPPOSITE This rug is of great sentimental value to us. It is the first thing I bought for Hugh when he employed me as his interior decorator, which is how I met him many years ago. We have restored it several times and the room is built around its colours.

'It's a tradition for us to have a full jar
of Quality Street at home. My friend Jess
gave me the wonderful picture made from
their wrappers that sits behind the jar.
Such a great present!'

Sir John Astley, BE
at Newmarket

'Aunt Corise was a great character, and a lot of her paintings are hanging in this room, pictures that I have known all my life. I loved her house and her use of reds, yellows, and blues.'

Dining Room

'I started by wallpapering the room. The design comes from the endpapers of a set of books I had years ago.'

This room was also the dining room for the previous owners, and we made very few changes to it. It was a more formal space in their day, but I wanted it to have a friendly feel because our kitchen does not have room to sit more than six people, so we have to use the dining room quite often if people come to lunch.

I started by wallpapering the room. The design comes from the endpapers of a set of books I had years ago, and a friend of mine who does digital wallpaper made it for me. It's a squiggle pattern that's hard to date, and one of those magic prints that work in any colour. I chose a warming green and red colourway as it's a north-facing room. It's also the sort of pattern that works really well with pictures. I had bought a John Bratby oil painting of fruit, and this also decided the colour palette for the room. I then made some heavy curtains from sage-green Melton wool, thinking I needed to keep the room warm, but they are rarely drawn as the windowsill invariably has plants on it.

When we first moved in I bought an antique dining table – it was that type of 'brown furniture' that nowadays goes for nothing at auction. The table was D-ended and too narrow for the room. It somehow made it rather depressing, so I stuck a large tablecloth on it. We had a lot of friends for Christmas that year and the table was covered with decorations, when Billy, our Sealyham terrier, decided to jump on and walk down it. The whole table dipped, and everything slipped into the middle.

But the festive dog disaster provided the perfect excuse to get rid of my mistake, and I decided to build a table strong enough for dogs to walk on (and for people to jump on, too). It is rock solid. The room is quite square, so I made the table wide enough for two or even three people to sit either end, and it works well for twelve or fourteen, though often it is just eight. It is quite nice having a modern table, as the previous one did tend to make the room feel like an old person's dining room. We now use the room much more.

If we don't want to be too smart, I just have an old Indian tablecloth, rush placemats, lots of flowers, and all kinds of decorative bits and pieces. But if I want to make it feel like quite a formal occasion, I put on a white tablecloth and put out all my best china and glasses. The big investment was ordering the set of lovely red chairs with leather seats. They are very comfortable, and though they are smart, they also have a sense of fun about them, which has completely lightened the room.

It is a very friendly place to sit and the acoustics are good because of the big heavy curtains. I have a serious problem when it comes to collecting old china, and I buy far too much. Part of the reason I can't resist constantly adding to my collection is that I get a lot of inspiration from it – from all the painting, and the patterns, and the different colours. Having such a quantity, I was lucky to find a great sideboard with an open bottom shelf, so piles of it are stored under there. I have my eye on some modern leaf plates and am wondering how I can find the space.

'I have a serious problem when it comes to
collecting old china, and I buy far too much.
I get a lot of inspiration from it – from all
the painting, and the patterns, and
the different colours.'

Office

'I am obsessed with books on old Irish houses and found a picture in one of the perfect scarlet room, so I copied the colour as best I could.'

The office is a small but very sunny room that is, in effect, a passage room that links the telly room to the kitchen. It has a lovely view out onto the terrace. We haven't changed it much, keeping the tall, boarded storage cupboards, but adding more bookshelves. I am obsessed with books on old Irish houses and found a picture in one of the perfect scarlet room. I wanted a red room somewhere in the house, so I copied the colour as best I could. I love the combination of red and white so I painted all the bookcases our house white, and then had a pair of very plain white modern desks made to fit. On the windows, there are some simple white Holland blinds.

As the room is so sunny, the blinds are often half down and the windowsill is a perfect resting place for geraniums in the winter. People are rather impressed that Hugh and I share an office, but in truth my desk is a dumping ground for my post and I tend to work at the kitchen table. I have tried not to crowd the room with pictures so as to have a bit of breathing space.

'The photograph over the desk is a scan from a book that shows the house as it was in the 1930s. Though it hasn't changed much, it's amazing to see how many more trees there are now.'

Kitchen

'I just wanted our kitchen to be as simple and as timeless as possible.'

The kitchen is one of the few rooms where we made some structural changes, opening up a couple of doors that had previously been blocked off, which reconnected the room to a back entrance and loo. We also opened up a door to what had been the laundry, and this became the perfect washing-up room. I love the kitchen, but it has quite a low ceiling and on a dark day you need the lights on. But opening up the doors has allowed extra light in and gives the room a more airy feel. We also have French windows leading out to the terrace, which we open whenever we can.

We inherited an Aga and had it re-enamelled in black, and we kept the stone overmantel and tidied it up. There is a big stone fireplace and beautiful old flagstones on the floor – the kitchen floor is one of the reasons I fell in love with the house. There is also a good larder room with slate shelves and lots of storage. It is painted in the lightest blue gloss because I have never forgotten being told that you should paint a larder pale blue to keep the flies away. We are lucky to have lots of other storage space in the back passage too, which helps prevent the kitchen from becoming too cluttered.

The room was once upon a time a chapel, and has a curious semi-circular end to it. We made new units that had to fit in a sweep along the curve, with very simple traditional doors made by our builders, and worktops made from honed Welsh slate. It's all very simple, with both the units and the walls painted in my favourite white gloss. I like keeping the bones of a kitchen simple and adding colour with things like china and tablecloths – all of which can be easily changed.

The table is the centre of the room. It's a very plain, 1960s scrubbed-pine table on loan from a great friend. It's something I am very fond of, as I have sat around it all my life in her family's kitchen. Both of us happened to be looking for tables at the same time, and she had always liked the long dining table from our old house, so we did a swap.

Having once had a house with a big kitchen-sitting room in the basement (in which we lived and never seemed to use the rest of the house), I did not want our new kitchen to end up as a sitting room. I did, however, want to make it cosy. I had a set of modern Windsor chairs that I had had made by a craftsman in Devon for our old kitchen. They are

big and incredibly comfortable, and I wanted to use them again. Though we could only fit six around the table, I decided it was no bad thing. If we have more than six people eating with us, it forces us to use our dining room or, if it's summer, to go outside to eat in the garden.

I'm obsessed with tablecloths and love laying the table even when we are on our own. Over the years I have collected lots of hand-blocked prints, but have recently been making up cloths and napkins from designs made by my Joy of Print studio. At the moment I have a thing about black and white, and have used this colourway to create hand-drawn stripes, checks and sunflower patterns with splashes of yellow.

Some time ago, I bought up a lot of plain white everyday china and use that mixed with sets of old plates, very simple glasses, and vintage steel cutlery from our local market. The table changes the whole time, and its scrubbed pine top works equally well with no cloth and classic rush placemats. The mats remind me of home and shops like Habitat and David Mellor in the 1970s – the style is still a big influence on me.

'I like keeping the bones of a kitchen simple and adding colour with things like china and tablecloths – all of which can be easily changed.'

There are only a few pictures in here, as I didn't want the room becoming too cluttered, which is all too easy to do in a kitchen. They are all quite strong images. There is an orange-and-black abstract print by Breon O'Casey, and either side of the sink are two Chris Ofili tea towels in simple Perspex frames. The rest of the colour comes from the cushions on the chairs.

In the winter the kitchen is the cosiest room in the house. We often have the stove lit and I bring out some old red velvet curtains to hang at the French windows. I bought them from the local market during a cold spell a few years ago as an emergency measure and they still come out each autumn. I will eventually get around to replacing them. In the summer we open both doors to the terrace and have breakfast outside, which is a treat. The dogs love being in here, in their baskets by the Aga, and I often use the kitchen table to work at, so it's pretty much the centre of the house.

OPPOSITE The kitchen is painted entirely in white gloss to keep the room as light and simple as possible. In contrast, there is a black Aga, slate worktops, and ebony chairs, with splashes of colour in the pictures and cushions.

Utility Room

'I loved the sink below the Gothic window. It gave the feeling of a lovely, old-fashioned washroom.'

This room was the utility room for the people who lived here before us, and they had their washing machine in it. What I loved about it was the sink beneath the Gothic window. Though we had to take the original sink out, the draining board had been there forever. It had this feel of a lovely, old-fashioned washroom and that was the atmosphere I wanted to keep. I also wanted the storage to look as though it had always been there, so I built a cupboard into the gap above the original radiator. I have this thing about Formica, which must be from my childhood, so I added a strip of yellow Formica to the units opposite – a sliver of yellow that I quite love and which gives it a slightly modern look. With the old tops above, however, it also has the feeling that it might always have been there. The dishwasher is in here as well as all the plates, china, and glass. Keeping everything in one place off the kitchen is really useful. The walls are covered in shiny paint. I love white shiny paint in utility rooms.

OPPOSITE We built a slim but practical glass cupboard over the radiator. I faced the shelves in white plastic lace, nailed on with white drawing pins.

OPPOSITE Some of the endless vases and jugs I have collected over the years. Many are from car boot sales and charity shops.

Dog Room

Life is Merrier

With a

Lakeland Terrier

'When I found the giant, shiny, white chest of drawers in a junk shop it was the perfect fit. It's now crammed with tea towels, my endless collection of hot water bottles (with their Cath Kidston covers), and even more dog stuff.'

'The back hall, lined with the coats, is a dark room, so I painted it ochre yellow and hung up my "weather" prints to cheer it up.'

Due to the way the house is laid out we have two back doors: one opens into a hall used to store coats and boots, and the other opens into the utility room (or 'the dog room' as we call it). This room was originally a kitchen for the old flat, so I had space to put a large sink under the window and can hide all the dog stuff away underneath it. I built it on a brick frame, made a thick iroko worktop as a double draining board, and added a couple of drawers. This sink gets used the whole time to wash the dogs, and for the laundry. The iroko bleaches down beautifully with time.

Everything in the dog room is coated in gloss white. We needed a new floor so I found some inexpensive slate tiles that are very practical. I also have a collection of dog pictures in here I'm very fond of. Some belonged to my father when he was a child, and this felt like the right home for them. I like a space like this to be really quite plain and functional, so when I found a giant, shiny, white chest of drawers in a junk shop, it was the perfect fit. It's now crammed with tea towels, my endless collection of hot water bottles (with their Cath Kidston covers), and even more dog stuff.

The back hall, lined with the coats, is a dark room, so I painted it ochre yellow and hung up my 'weather' prints above the coat rack to cheer it up. It has the original black-and-terracotta tiled floor, which is perfect with all the boots coming in and out. This room has a glass door leading into a small back passage, which I painted a strong salmon pink to contrast with the yellow.

It was a tremendous luxury to have a room with big cupboards to store our coats and all the dog stuff. There was so much storage space in the house when we arrived, but I was shocked by how quickly it filled up – it must be my magpie instincts. It's all too easy to gather clutter so I have to be very strict and clear things out. The hardest challenge is getting rid of sentimental gifts that don't fit in. I find it very difficult to throw these things out and they tend to get stuffed into drawers, but I am getting more ruthless. As my tastes changed over the years, I learnt to sell things I used to hold on to even when I was no longer fond of them. I had a huge collection of red-and-white kitchenware, for example, that I sold when we moved and haven't regretted it. I really don't want to end up in a cluttered house.

'I decided to save most of my chintz and flowers for the attic, and give the first-floor a modern country-house feel.'

This part of the house feels very connected to the ground floor. The staircase climbs up to the first-floor landing, where banisters look down over the inner hall below. The space is lit by a large skylight. When we arrived, the landing at the top of the first flight of stairs had a partition that hid a glass light well to the passage below. I took this out, opening it up, so now the landing has enough room for a table and lamp. It has a good feeling of space, which you even appreciate downstairs.

Bookshelves are my favourite form of decoration. I like the way they introduce colour and, as I buy far more books than I could possibly read, I needed more bookcases in the house and built one here across the back wall. Since there is a wall of colourful pictures on the hall stairs, I felt the upstairs landing needed to feel a bit calmer, so I have tried to be very disciplined with what I have hung here. There are a simple pair of mirrors either side of the bookshelves and a large picture by my sister, of Stanley our dog. She commissioned his portrait made out of balloons, and photographed it, so he now hangs larger than life on the back wall. Our bedroom is up another half landing, also with a view over the hall, so I added more bookshelves and cupboards to tie it all in.

The view across the landings is dominated by the large paper lanterns we have hanging in a cluster over the stairwell. Outside our bedroom, I have hung a framed blanket made to celebrate twenty years of Cath Kidston. It tells the story of the company in embroidery and knitting, and was given to me as a surprise. It must have been painstaking to put together, each letter having been cut out by hand, and the two girls who made it for me stitched their signatures at the bottom of it to read 'Slaved away by Jess and Lulu'! It's my favourite memento from those years.

As so many rooms lead off it, I made the first-floor hall purposely plain, painting it our house white. Our two main guest bedrooms are on this floor. As their doors are often left open, they need to link well, so I decided to save most of my chintz and flowers for the attic. The bedrooms have decent proportions, and I liked the idea of them having a modern country-house feel – quite simple and unfussy, while at the same time warm and welcoming. I have used quite a lot of yellow, which connects to the colour of the stair carpet. I haven't used much print except in our bedroom and dressing room. The main floral touches here are pots of geraniums, and the flowers I put out when people come to stay.

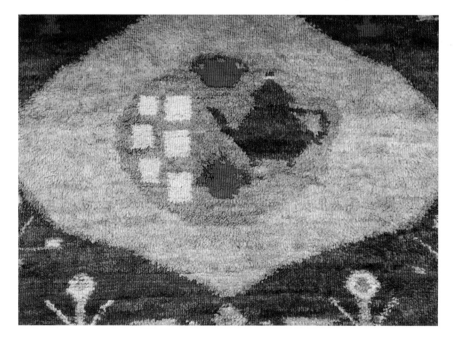

'I used three large classic paper lanterns grouped like a bunch of balloons. They hang on red cord and add a sense of fun to the hall.'

Castle Bedroom

'My sister gave me a wonderful piece of printed cotton from Pondicherry, which is pinned over the headboard.'

This room sits above the kitchen and has the same semi-circular wall at one end, with three sash windows providing a view out to the chickens. At the opposite end there is another large window looking out onto the terrace, so it's light and airy. The room started out with lining paper on the walls, but my inspiration came from a collection of photographs and prints of pink and red rooms that I had been keeping in an 'ideas' file gathered from Pinterest, old books, and magazines. I needed to have this room ready for our first Christmas in the house, so I ordered pale-pink linen curtains that I knew would be quite versatile. I painted the floorboards white and added a rug of the same wool carpet that is in the other bedrooms, and this was the way it stayed for the first year.

Before we left our old house, Hugh photographed pretty much everything we had, so from these pictures I was able to sort things into groups, working out what might fit where in our new home. This gave me some order when I was unpacking and it was invaluable to work this way. The room is a mixture of bits and pieces I had collected that go roughly together, and then I bought various things where I needed to fill a space.

I had a bed, old bedside tables, lamps, and a desk from my grandmother, all of which fitted. I also had some chairs with red covers I could use, and added a new orange-and-pink Moroccan rug I couldn't resist. Sometimes I find something like the rug and have no idea where it will fit, so I have to try it around the house until it finds a home. Usually it's a picture, or something I've spotted on an auction site. It's not an ideal way to work, but it does give the house a more 'eclectic' look.

When the rug ended up in this bedroom, I started to introduce more colour. My sister gave me a wonderful piece of printed cotton from Pondicherry, which is pinned over the headboard, while another friend gave me an orange striped blanket, and so the picture began to build. I had got used to the lining paper colour in the room and liked it, but wanted some sort of pattern on the walls. My neighbour, the designer Sarah Hardaker, who can custom print her designs to order, had a wallpaper printed on a base to match the lining paper. The result is a very faded large-scale pattern that just breaks up the walls – it looks like the tracing of an old Chinese paper. I also felt I needed a set of pictures that would bring some order to the room, so I commissioned the artist Henrietta Molinaro to make me a digital set, in my perfect red, of her classic blue cyanotype flower prints. I also found some beautiful printed paper lampshades from Rosi de Ruig to bring a bit more colour into the room.

The most striking thing is the way the bath sits in the centre of the semi-circular end of the room. I am not really a fan of baths in bedrooms (they remind me of boutique hotel rooms), and I find myself apologising for it when I show guests the room. Some people love it and others look positively alarmed. The fact was that the bathroom off the room is very small and only fits a shower, so it made sense to use the extra space in the bedroom for the bath. However, I am toying with the idea of building some sort of low wall, or finding the perfect screen to hide it... One way or another, as it stands there is a great view of the chickens from the bath!

'Sometimes I find something and have no idea where it will fit, so I have to try it around the house until it finds a home... It's not an ideal way to work, but it does give the house a more "eclectic" look.'

Fish Bedroom

'Once the key pieces of a room are in place and it is comfortable, I like to take time to finish it off, as it's the layers that really make a space.'

This spare room sits on the corner of the house over the dining room with a large window facing north west towards the garden. It gets the sun in the morning, which can be rather annoying for anyone trying to have a lie in, so I gave it thick interlined curtains to keep the light out. The colours of the room were decided by an enormous theatre backdrop that dominates the neighbouring bathroom – a fantastic scene of swimming fish in blues and yellows.

It is a cosy bedroom despite its high ceilings and lack of sunlight. I do think of comfort first when decorating a bedroom, so I splashed out on a large comfortable double bed and headboard. I have used simple white linen sheets and traditional wool blankets from Lancashire in the main spare rooms – I like the feeling of sheets and blankets (instead of a duvet) as a treat. As much as I love print, I prefer plain sheets but have a huge collection of patterned pillowcases to top them off. I love the original patterns from brands like D. Porthault, which are eye-wateringly expensive, so I have collected the baby pillowcases from their sales over the years. My favourite comes in a print they licensed from Matisse, which they still make today.

I had to make a decision on the bedroom carpets in a hurry – we were moving in in time for Christmas and were expecting a full house. Floorboards weren't an option and I hadn't really worked out the colour schemes for the bedrooms at that time. The decorator John Fowler used to use a cream, almost flat, shag pile carpet in his bedrooms and I wanted that look, so I chose what I thought was similar from a small swatch. We accidentally ended up with the deepest wool pile carpet you have ever seen. It's nothing like I expected and totally impractical, but it's here to stay.

The room is painted a mid-blue and dressed with yellow curtains, so I covered the chairs in shades of deep pink to warm things up and added some geometric cushions from Fine Cell Work – this is a wonderful charity teaching prisoners needlework, who produce the most incredible range of hand-stitched cushions. I bought an old chintz sofa for the end of the bed that needs re-covering. I have tried endless swatches and not found 'the one'. It may take years before it gets done, but I rather love the imperfection of it not being quite right.

Once the key pieces of a room are in place and it is comfortable, I like to take time to finish it off, as it's the layers that really make a space. It is also much more affordable this way. It took a few years to find the oil painting over the fireplace but I think it was worth the wait. The final touch when I have guests staying is to put flowers by the bed, geraniums on the windowsill, and some good books either side of the bed.

OPPOSITE The fish bedroom ended up in my default colour palette of pink, blue, and yellow. I had the pink chair already and added a yellow rug and curtains.

'As much as I love print, I prefer plain sheets but have a huge collection of patterned pillowcases to top them off.'

Fish Bathroom

'I found the fish painting in one of my favourite antique shops. It made my heart stop when I walked in and saw it.'

As the original house had more bedrooms than we needed, we were able to convert a couple into large bathrooms and this is one of them. The fish painting sets the whole mood for this room, which is the bathroom I like best in the house. I found the fish painting in one of my favourite antique shops in the Lillie Road in west London. It made my heart stop when I walked in and saw it hanging over the stairs, then I saw the red sold sticker. An American dealer had just been in and bought it. I was lucky as it turned out they wanted to sell it on and I was able to do a deal before it was whisked off to their shippers. It was a close thing. It is an underwater scene for a theatre backdrop and it is enormous, about two metres wide. Of course, it cost far, far more to frame than it did to buy and only just fitted though the door.

We salvaged the original cast-iron bath from the master bathroom as it's huge and very comfortable. With its slightly deco feel it set the look for the rest of the bathrooms in the house. I thought it would be good to make all of the bathrooms feel like they had always been here, so I used old-fashioned taps everywhere and panelled the bath on all sides in honed Carrara marble. As the fish picture dominates the room, everything else had to fit around it. I ended up using a favourite trellis wallpaper in a clean yellow-and-white colourway, and brought in some blue with a rug by the bath. The floor is just a plain white lino and I painted the original shutters white to match. The last things I found were two 1960s chairs in bright yellow with rush seats, which fit with the character of the room.

christopher corr

Dressing Room

'It's a room full of memories with my old family pictures.'

The dressing room is the only other room on the first floor with windows looking down the valley. It sits sandwiched between our bedroom and bathroom, so, as well as being a practical room where I have all my clothes and my dressing table, it feels very private. It's also the room where I keep my favourite family photographs, as I don't like putting these around the house. They are propped up on the mantelpiece, and in old frames on the chest of drawers. I keep some under glass on my dressing table – I copied this idea from my mother as it was something that intrigued me as a child.

There are portraits of my grandmother, Iso Pease, and great-aunt, Myrtle McGowan, as children in here, as well as one of my late brother. The rest of the pictures are old engravings that I had in my first flat and which needed a home, and I thought the colours worked well in the room. It's a room full of memories and is very peaceful. It's a favourite quiet place to lie and read a book or work on my laptop when I don't want to be disturbed.

OPPOSITE A day bed covered in a tomato-red quilt sits under family portraits. This is the quietest room in the house and the best place to read.

I needed cupboards, but I didn't want them to dominate, so I built them down the length of the room, with an opening in the middle giving access to the bathroom. They are flat-faced, with a cornice and skirting running top and bottom, and because they are wallpapered in the same paper as the rest of the room they disappear into it. I used the same Birds and Roses design as the bedroom curtains. I don't generally like things to be too matching, but these rooms are so connected that in this case it made sense. I sprayed the wallpaper on the doors with shoe-guard to protect it and, as the doors are on touch latches with no handles, I added some plain glass finger plates.

To keep things a little more contemporary, I used a modern white chest of drawers and a circular mirror over the fireplace. I have left the windows without curtains and just use the beautiful shutters and the cream Holland blinds to block out the sun. The window seats have pale-blue squab cushions. I covered a chaise longue in a tomato-red quilt from Zara Home, and used the same red on the window seats in our bedroom to give more continuity to the rooms. I like the way red lifts a room. If I'm up early and don't want to disturb Hugh, I come in here.

The final thing I found for this room was a chandelier. I had never thought of owning one before, but I fell in love with this one as soon as I saw it in an antique shop in Fulham. It has beautiful pink, yellow, and blue glass in it, which was perfect for the room. I managed to persuade Hugh to buy it for me for Christmas.

OPPOSITE The portraits here show my grandmother and aunt as children. We discovered my grandmother's portrait hidden behind mirrored glass. She was probably like me and didn't like looking at her own image!

Master Bedroom

'I used to decorate other people's houses in a very decisive way, but in my own home it can take me ages to make decisions. The endless problem-solving is one of the reasons I love decorating.'

I was intrigued by this house from the moment I first set eyes upon it, but it was when we came into this room and I saw the view from the windows looking down the valley that I was smitten. You can see for miles without glimpsing another house. There is a beautiful wood of beech trees to the right and the fields slope away into the distance. To have such a view from our bedroom was too good to be true.

The room itself is lovely and open, very light, with three tall windows, each with shutters and window seats. It sits at the front of the house, up half a flight of stairs, and is set away from the other bedrooms. Originally it was probably two rooms, as it is divided by an arch, and though we could have taken this out, it seemed part of the character, so we decided to leave it. For some reason, I was quite daunted by how to decorate this room, so I left it until last, and still feel it is very much a work in progress. Structurally, the one thing I did know was that I wanted to remove a wall of modern cupboards and put in a fireplace. I was lucky that an antique-dealer friend found me a pretty painted one at auction that fitted the space perfectly and gave a focus to the room.

My starting point for the decoration was the colours. I worked out a palette of lemon yellow, soft blues, and faded tomato reds, which was inspired by some pictures I already had. These included a framed colourful silk headscarf, decorated with a painting by Picasso, that was exactly the right size for over the fireplace, and a bright yellow picture by Terry Frost that hangs opposite. It's said not to be a good idea to have bright colours in a bedroom (it's not meant to be restful), so the walls are painted in a soothing shade of gentle pale blue. The rest of the pictures are once again mainly a mix of what we had gathered over the years.

At first I thought we should not have curtains in the bedroom and just use the shutters as they are beautiful in here. I then felt the room needed warming up, so I decided to use my favourite Birds and Roses material from my old business. It has an old-fashioned feel, which I like, especially since most of the pictures I have used in the room are quite modern. It provided a good contrast, and I liked the fact that the curtains were not very fashionable and looked like they had always belonged there.

The challenge has been the furniture. I had nothing quite right for a room of this size, apart from a couple of yellow and blue chests of drawers, and I have dithered over the bed. I started out with a simple white linen headboard and valance. It looked really dull, so I covered the headboard with a red-and-white striped linen in an attempt to cheer it up. I have finally decided however that what it really needs is a four-poster bed, something with a very simple frame, probably painted lemon yellow, and not too draped in curtains. Hopefully it will pull the room together. I now need to measure it up and check if the proportions will work.

The rest of the furniture in this room is painted, and I bought a pair of white bedside tables. I covered a small sofa in yellow for the end of the bed, and also had space for an armchair. I have been searching for a tall painted bookcase to replace the table to the left of the fireplace. Last but not least, I need to find the right rug. When I ran my interior design business, I used to be able to decorate other people's houses in a very decisive way, but in my own home it can take me ages to make decisions. Perhaps the endless problem-solving is one of the reasons I love decorating.

'I did commission one piece for the room. When Hugh and I got married, the artist Rob Ryan made a beautiful paper cut of our last house, and, as I love his work, to celebrate moving in here I asked him to make one of Paradise. It hangs above our bed, along with a poem that he wrote specially.'

Master Bathroom

'I went on a sweep round the house searching for blue and white, gathering up anything from plant pots to dishes, and then I styled up the room.'

When I was sorting through all the photographs that Hugh had taken of our belongings and was wondering what could go where in the house, I realised that I had a group of blue and white pictures and china that needed to stay together. Though I didn't want a traditional blue and white bathroom, I liked the idea of mixing blues and turquoise as the Greeks do so well. Once again I started with a white room, and then went on a sweep round the house searching for blue and white, gathering up anything from plant pots to dishes, and then I styled up the room. I don't usually decorate a room in one colour, but I liked the idea of a simple clean-looking bathroom, and it was a good way of using up what I had. We go to Greece each summer, so I started bringing back turquoise Greek beads each year, along with tin decorations, so the room has really ended up with a holiday feel.

To add to the look, I recently lined our glass medicine cabinet in a blue and white pattern from my Joy of Print studio. I just printed it onto A4 sheets of paper to fit each pane of glass, and I love the results. There were gaps in the room to begin with, but it's been fun looking out for more pictures and choosing new materials. I had space for an armchair, which I covered in a plain pale-blue linen. The most useful piece is a laundry box, bought from our local auction house, which doubles as a stool, and is now upholstered in a beautiful blue and white block print. I also had a basin stand made like an old-fashioned sideboard, with a marble top. It has drawers and cupboards and is perfect for hiding all my bits and pieces. A large antique mirror hangs over the basin to finish things off. Though it is quite a tidy room, I need to control my urge to buy any more odds and ends for it before it starts getting cluttered.

OPPOSITE The bathroom is strongly influenced by my love of Greece. I like the way the Greeks decorate and mix different blues together so well.

'I wanted to give it a feeling of things that I remembered from my childhood, which is why we have the budgie wallpaper up here.'

I love the attic. When you come up the top stairs, there is a wonderful feeling of surprise as it unfurls much further than one expects. It also feels strangely larger than the floor below. There are four bedrooms and two bathrooms up here, all beautifully light. It is where we can spread out when we have a lot of friends to stay, and we can close it off completely when we are quiet. The attic is all about children, families, Christmas, those kinds of things. A couple of the rooms have pairs of single beds, which give it a nursery atmosphere. I wanted to give it a feeling of all the things that I remembered from my childhood, and it is the place where it felt right to use all my old chintz and patterned wallpapers.

The people who were living here before had made the attic into a separate flat for a lodger. When we arrived it was completely unspoilt and had these old linen cupboards, which for me were almost reason enough to buy the house. When we came to restore this floor, it felt important to retain as many of the original features as we could. We have kept the cleaning cupboard, with its old housekeeper's sink and draining board, pretty much as it was – save for redoing the plumbing and replacing the taps with similar old-fashioned ones. The original linen cupboard is now bursting full with my endless collection of sheets and pillowcases. We also managed to re-use the old pine clothes cupboards, painting them white, and we even kept some of the (rather school-style) 1950s sinks, leaving one in a bedroom. Where we needed new cupboards, our builders were able to make them look like they had always been there.

The bedrooms run off two different passages. The first is painted pale blue, tying in with the walls of the staircase from the first floor, but where you turn into the second passage, separated by a doorway, I have papered the walls in a rather eccentric budgerigar print, which I found on the internet. It reminds me of my childhood and carries the nursery feel to this end of the attic.

Some of the rooms are carpeted, with the boards left painted around the edge. In my haste to move in, I chose an apple-green wool carpet for the passages. This is the one thing I want to change. The colour just doesn't work with the rest of the decoration, and it was a very costly mistake. I am bracing myself to replace it.

To balance all the old fixtures and fittings I have used quite clean colours up here, such as pinks and strong blues set against white. Where I have used chintz, I have kept the rooms simple and added things like colourful block-printed cushions and rugs. I have also hung quite a few of my modern pictures up here to prevent it all looking too nostalgic. Where I have used rolls of rose wallpaper in a bathroom, I have purposely kept the floorboards plain white to keep the room looking fresh. Above all, I wanted the attic to be a friendly, cosy part of the house for children when they come to stay, and I hope that they will have their own memories of rose-papered bedrooms and budgie wallpaper in years to come.

'We have kept the cleaning cupboard, with its old housekeeper's sink and draining board, pretty much as it was – save for redoing the plumbing and replacing the taps with similar old-fashioned ones.'

Spare Bedroom

The main spare room in the attic sits at the top of the stairs, with dormer windows on two sides. In one direction there is a view over the driveway and garden, and in the other, over the chickens. The attic is quite high up so the room feels like it is almost above the tree line, which I love. The room is a decent size but, with its low sloping ceilings, feels rather snug.

The first thing I did was to order a large comfortable bed. I had a favourite painted table with a fox's face carved on it, which has travelled with me from place to place over the years. My friend William Yeoward had always coveted it, so I did a deal with him that, in return for a new one, he could copy it for his collection. So now I have a pair that have ended up here as bedside tables. I have a passion for white china lamps and found two decorated with china flowers to go on top of the tables.

Some furnishing linen, which I had squirrelled away from the business, was used for the bedhead and to re-cover an old sofa. This set the colours for the room as blue, pink, and green, which were offset with lots of white. I had the wallpaper, which is the same pattern as that used in the fish bathroom, custom made in a special colour. I didn't see it until it was up and it was much brighter than I expected, so we painted a wash of white glaze over it to tone it down.

When it came to hanging pictures, once again it was a case of using up ones that I had, such as an oil painting of hydrangeas by Aunt Corise, and some antique French engravings in their original green mounts, inherited from my parents. I made one big mistake, which was to lay a faded emerald-green carpet down. Though we lived with it for four years, it just wasn't quite right, and in the end I bit the bullet and changed it for a simple cream wool carpet. Suddenly the whole room fell into place. I added a pink chair and a few modern bits and pieces, and that's how it is today. Friends tell me it's a lovely room to sleep in.

'I had the wallpaper custom made in a special colour. I didn't see it until it was up and it was much brighter than I expected, so we painted a wash of white glaze over it to tone it down.'

Messel Bedroom

I call this the 'Messel bedroom' as the chintz on the beds is by Oliver Messel, the famous 20th-century stage designer. It is very precious to me and I came across it in a rather roundabout way. When I was young, I spent a lot of time with my grandmother. She had a beautiful house and my love of decorating and fabrics was inherited from her. She would come to London and take me to a magical material shop called Afia Fabrics, just off Baker Street. Run by Mr and Mrs Victor Afia, they had been open since the 1930s, importing the best furnishing fabric from all over Europe.

I loved rifling around, and Heather, who worked for them, would allow me to explore their basement store, which housed all the old rolls of fabric. There were incredible toile de jouy and end-of-line chintzes to be found and, in amongst them, rare Oliver Messel fabrics. When I went on to get a job as assistant to Nicky Haslam, I would go and buy them for his projects. The fabrics in the basement of Afia were a huge influence on me – and when I started Cath Kidston they were also a source of stock for the shop. My first ironing board covers, for example, were made from Afia fabrics. Sadly the shop closed some years ago, and I wish I had bought up more of the stock at the time.

Soon after we had bought the house, out of the blue I got a letter from Heather (whom I hadn't heard from for years). She had discovered a roll of Messel fabric and asked if I would be interested in it. The fabric turned out to be the exquisite bouquets of flowers that are on the bed today. As it's my dream chintz, I wondered how on earth I had missed it all those years ago. The material is so bright and colourful it dominates the room, and I had just enough for bedheads and valances.

I whitewashed the walls and kept the decoration very simple, just a pair of single children's beds, white painted floors, and a plain green rug. I also added the same white shutters as I had in the other bedrooms. On the walls I have hung modern pictures. I collect the work of my talented goddaughter, Rose Electra Harris, and have a number of her prints. I also added some china by the ceramicist Polly Fern, as the colours seemed fun against the white. There are a couple of colourful cushions and some striped Moroccan blankets. When I made the bedheads and valances I felt rather guilty about cutting up the Messel fabric. Recently Heather contacted me to say she had found another piece. It is now in tissue paper in a bottom drawer, saved for posterity.

'When I was young, I spent a lot of
time with my grandmother. She had a
beautiful house and my love of decorating
and fabrics was inherited from her.'

Attic Bathroom

'When people come to stay, I always put out giant white bath towels and treats like pine bath essence, as well as favourite soaps and, of course, a geranium on the windowsill.'

I always wanted to have a children's bathroom in the house, and this is it. I put in an enormous bath, and when we have small children staying there are sometimes four babies in it at a time. They can then get dry on the sofa, which has a giant towel over the seat. Although it has the appearance of a children's room, with the huge bath and sofa, it's very comfortable for adults.

The room has an unashamedly old-fashioned feel to it. I used the original basin and panelled the bath in white glass, an idea that I remembered from my childhood. I kept the tiny fireplace in the corner and took a pine cupboard from another room to fit the other side. The room is dominated by a wallpaper called Paris Rose, one I designed some years ago at Cath Kidston, which was inspired by an old French dress fabric. I have always loved those big floral prints on furnishings. A lot of old wallpaper documents have a gloss finish, so I varnished the paper in here as it brings out the colours and is also practical in a bathroom. The white sofa has cushions from my friend, Molly Mahon, whose block-printed designs I very much admire. The floor is painted white with a colourful Indian dhurrie, so despite the nostalgic feel in here, it is still fresh.

OPPOSITE The sink and mirror were original to the attic part of the house. We kept as many of these old fittings as we could.

Attic Twin

'I had a pile of lustreware plates I had been collecting for ages, so I hung them on the wall above the beds.'

This is the room we use when children stay or we are full to the brim. It sits at the far end of the attic, the part that was once a separate flat before we arrived. To get to it you pass through the 'budgie' passage. I love this wallpaper, which I found online and just couldn't resist. It reminded me of my childhood as we had a budgie at home – it was very fashionable in the 1960s. It also takes me back to the sort of patterns in the old wallpaper sample books I used to buy at car boot sales for inspiration. Anyway, I loved the colours, and the design, and the chirpiness of it all. The attic passage seemed the one place I could get away with such a bold choice.

It meant that when it came to decorating the twin room off the passage I needed to choose something rather calmer. I love pink and yellow together, so I had bright yellow bedheads and valances made and used my pink and white bedlinen. The room started out white but seemed a bit cold, so I papered it with a tiny grey-and-white pattern I designed and had made for me by my friend John Mark, who has a digital printing company. I had a pile of lustreware plates I had been collecting for ages, so I hung them on the wall above the beds. I need to collect more to finish it off but that will happen in time. I also have my eye out for a pair of sugar-pink eiderdowns.

OPPOSITE I like the combination of grey and yellow so had the wallpaper custom-printed. I copied the pattern from the border of an old Indian tablecloth and scaled it up to work as a print.

'I have always loved pink and yellow together and like the way the colours lift the room.'

'The wood has ancient beech trees and, at the right time of year, is filled with ferns and bluebells.'

There is an ancient feel to the land around us. The house sits on a hill looking down the valley. There is a beech wood to one side, and within the trees there is a large Iron Age burial mound, which you can see clearly in the winter. Above the house and across a road, the land rises up to meet the Cotswold Way. Here there are remains of a timeworn fort, and views from the beacon across to the Severn Bridge and for miles into mid-Wales. It's a favourite place to take the dogs, particularly at the beginning and end of the day when it is deserted. The fact that the fort and burial mound date back to ancient times, and that there is a stream running through the woods providing water, suggests that there have been settlements here for ever. To this day, all of our water comes from a spring in the wood.

One of the things that really captured my heart when we found the house was its breathtaking position, and the simplicity of the view, with the land falling away down a steep bank straight to the meadows beyond. We can step down some old stone steps into the field, and from there we can walk in numerous directions. For a short walk we can also take a path into the woods, bringing us out at the bottom of the field, with a wonderful view back up to the house. The wood has ancient beech trees and, at the right time of year, it is filled with ferns and bluebells. There is a pond and a stream, which makes it a favourite with visiting children.

At our previous house we had had a very labour-intensive garden, so we wanted to keep things much simpler here. I liked the idea of the view being uninterrupted, so we have kept the front to an open lawn with simple planting next to the house. We started with a small terrace outside the kitchen, where we have a long table for eating out in the summer. To create more light, we took out a big cedar, which overhung the house and was quite oppressive, and replaced it with a catalpa. It became clear that the terrace was the sunny spot where we would spend most of our time, so we extended it, laying a wide area of Welsh pennant slabs broken up with gaps for planting. It is lovely looking out of the kitchen window and seeing all that we have done.

At the back of the house we inherited an orchard, which we added to, and underplanted with daffodils and tulips for the spring. I am always keen to have flowers to pick, so have worked out how to always have something pretty flowering. During the summer it is left to long grass with a mown path, so it is quite low maintenance. There is a border running down one side of the orchard, which I also treat like a cutting garden. It has lots of roses in high summer and plenty of dahlias later in the year.

As you drive up to the house, there was originally a wide expanse of gravel, which gave you the feeling you were arriving at a hotel. We made an oval lawn in the centre, surrounding a beech tree, and added some box for more green, while a red brick wall that looked out of place with the Cotswold stone is now hidden behind a yew hedge.

There is another steep bank behind the house, so tucked away up there we built a greenhouse and a chicken run. This is the working area where I also have a tiny kitchen garden. I put in the greenhouse to grow flowers I could use to bring the outside in, such as dahlias, sweet William, sweet peas, and my beloved geraniums. The garden is really all about the view, sitting out on the terrace, and the fact that pretty much all year round I am able to pick flowers for the house.

'I have kept the rest of the planting quite simple with white cistus, sage, lavender, and lady's mantle filling the gaps. I have also allowed small daisy plants to self-seed, which I may live to regret as they are already growing everywhere.'

Greenhouse

'Today, the first thing I do when I arrive home is bring some geraniums into the house and pick a bunch of flowers for the kitchen table.'

I have always been obsessed with having plants and flowers in the house. I am not a good gardener, but even as a child I loved picking flowers and was encouraged by my parents to have my own small patch of garden in which I probably grew things like marigolds and radishes. In my twenties, when I lived in a rented room in someone else's house, I would bring flowers up from the country, or keep geraniums near the windowsill in my bedroom. Today, the first thing I do when I arrive home is bring some geraniums into the house and pick a bunch of flowers for the kitchen table. It doesn't feel like home without them. If I arrive at the house after dark, I have even been known to go out with my torch and secateurs. Part of my plan for the garden was to always have something to pick all year round.

When we bought the house, there were surprisingly few outbuildings, other than a garage and a small hen house, so the first thing we did was to build a log shed, and put up a tiny lean-to greenhouse near the back door. It sat against the bank and didn't really get enough light, so I finally decided to order a proper traditional greenhouse to sit above the bank. It's not that large, but is perfect for all my plants and cuttings, and in winter, when they need protecting from the frost, it is full of geraniums. I have endless pink and red varieties, including a standard one that, staked, grows over a metre high and is great for bringing into the house. We also have jasmine and daturas, so it is often filled to bursting. Some people are wary of growing daturas, as they are poisonous. I am always very careful to keep them away from the dogs, but I love their big white bell flowers and the way they grow so tall. I love scented pelargoniums, and have also built up a collection of many mint and lemon-leaf plants; I even have some with leaves that smell of Coca Cola. With help I have started cultivating lots of cuttings – it's a matter of time before I run out of space. My challenge now is finding the right size pots for bringing them in, so I have been collecting 1960s white china cachepots, and old wicker pots whenever I can find them, the best places to look being car boot sales.

Much of the summer is spent watering, feeding, and deadheading the plants, and bringing a stream of pots in and out of the house. Most geraniums don't really like being indoors for too long, so I have to change them around, which is a labour

'I finally decided to order a proper traditional greenhouse to sit above the bank. It's not that large, but is perfect for all my plants and cuttings.'

of love, and a bank of them tend to pile up on the terrace awaiting their turn to be put back in the greenhouse. At this time of year it can be quite empty but as the frosts start they all head back in. Towards Christmas we have to make room for the paper-white bulbs (which have been sitting under the stairs) to get them ready for the house. Once they start to sprout, they get transferred into big china bowls and the earth is covered in moss. I make supports for them from hazel twigs picked in the wood. The other plants I love to grow are amaryllis, but the timing on these always catches me out. They often end up being ready months after Christmas and are a law unto themselves.

As the deer and rabbits come into the garden and eat what they can, we have fenced off a small area around the greenhouse to grow cutting flowers. This year it was packed with sweet Williams and anemones, which miraculously flowered well into the winter. I grow endless dahlias and sweet peas and also have a salad and herb patch. It has been fun to try new seeds each year.

My big extravagance is heating the greenhouse in the winter, but it does mean we have many more house plants available all year round. It really is a passion, I love spending time up here and just wish I had even more space.

Terrace

'The sun stays until the evening on the far end of the terrace, so I found an old-fashioned canvas swing seat to put against the wall. It's now the dogs' favourite sunbathing spot.'

The terrace fills a corner of the garden where the front of the house meets the side extension. It forms the main view from the kitchen and you can also walk out to it from the hall. It is an area we use throughout the summer as an outside room, but is also an integral part of the outlook from the side of the house we use every day. It is very sheltered and sunny, and at the far end has a wonderful view down the valley. It started out as a small paved area where the previous owners had their table and chairs outside the kitchen door. I was unsure how to alter it and when we came to the landscaping we were at the end of our budget, so I extended the area a little to make room for more chairs and left it at that. I soon realised it was the part of the garden we would use the most. I wanted a feeling of space and marked out a plan to extend it to fill the whole corner of the lawn. It looked enormous and I was worried that the view from the kitchen would just be an expanse of grey stone. I decided to stagger the edge of the paving where it met the lawn and leave space for the grass to grow around the outside paving stones. This way the hard edge would be broken up and blend in with the landscape, and the eye would be drawn out to the lawn and view beyond. I also decided to use old Welsh pennant paving slabs. The colour is softer than York stone and sits well with the Cotswold stone of the house. I laid out where there would be large spaces amongst the slabs for planting to break things up, taking into account where the furniture needed to go as the sun moves during the day, and the plan fell into place. Once the paving was laid, the first things I planted were some individual yew trees. They are still small, but I plan to clip them into squares as they grow so there is some shape and colour in winter. I have kept the rest of the planting quite simple with white cistus, sage, lavender, and lady's mantle filling the gaps. There are also herbs dotted around in some stone tubs and bay and rosemary against the wall. I have allowed small daisy plants to self-seed, which I may live to regret as they are already growing everywhere. Extra colour comes in the form of the rows of geranium pots that line up endlessly outside the kitchen door, getting some much needed sunshine before they are taken back in the house.

The furniture on the terrace is all quite simple. Close to the kitchen I have a long, rather rustic, wooden table and benches, enough to seat twelve.

I had planned for the furniture to sit under the shade of the catalpa tree, but it was too far from the kitchen door to be practical. Instead I moved it closer and bring out an umbrella when it's sunny. I have a pile of very faded, block-printed Indian bedcovers I have collected over the years, which I use as tablecloths. I pile geraniums on top when the table is not laid for eating. Luckily we planted the catalpa tree on the lawn pretty much as soon as we arrived and it's amazing how it has grown large enough in six years to offer really good shade. We put the chairs under it on a hot day. The sun stays until the evening on the far end of the terrace, so I found an old-fashioned canvas swing seat to put against the wall. It's now the dogs' favourite sunbathing spot. The only other furniture we have this end is an old stone bench and some Adirondack chairs with simple basket-weave canvas seat cushions. We sit and get a good view down the valley from here in the evenings.

The view out of the kitchen is much more cheery now with the planting to look out on and, aside from being very practical, the terrace hopefully blends in well with the simplicity of the rest of the garden and the landscape.

'I liked the idea of the paving drifting into the lawn and the eye being drawn across the grass to the view ahead.'

Summer Room

There is a separate building to the side of the house which was originally the coach house. The tracks are still visible in the field where in previous centuries carriages would have come around to drop people off. There was another family living there when we bought the house, but we have now taken it over and joined the properties as they once were. We use the space mainly for storage but have made a covered eating area on the side of the building and created a summer room. It's very cool, light, and airy over here and has a different feel to the main house, almost like a holiday home. Keeping the decorating simple, I whitewashed the room, and Dave, our wonderful builder, made two plain box sofa frames, each with a mattress seat on top. I joined them with a white cube to make a table in the corner. We then made another low box on wheels with a slate top to use as a coffee table.

I was brought up to be very aware of the decorator John Fowler, and his work was very influential to me. He used lime green and brown together beautifully and I have always loved the combination, which I have used here. I brought in an old brown sofa we had spare and kept the cushions green and brown – combining simple block prints from Molly Mahon and my Joy of Print studio, with brown-and-white striped Hungarian embroidery. There are modern lamps and pieces of wooden sculpture, which work well against the plain background. It almost has a 1960s feel in here. We inherited a wooden floor so I covered it in a green-and-white geometric cotton dhurrie we had at our old house. I fill the room with lemon-scented geraniums in the summer months and in the winter they huddle up safe from the frost on the windowsill.

OPPOSITE I love the combination of lime green and brown used in this room. The rose block print on the cushion is from my Joy of Print studio.

Acknowledgements

Many thanks to...

Helen Lewis, Lucy Smith, Alice Kennedy-Owen
and Katie Cowan from Pavilion Books for all their
support on the project, and to Krissy Mallett.

Elisabeth Lester, Joanne Sanders, Julie D'Anglesio,
and Mary Collier for their endless help too. Also
thanks to Christopher Simon Sykes, who was such
a pleasure to work with.

Finally thanks to Hugh for his patience.

Above all, to Dave Savage and his wonderful team
of builders, who helped put our house back together
with such care and attention to detail.